LOVE NOTES FROM THE HEART OF GOD

VICTORY IN JESUS

CHRISTA ERARIO

WestBow Press
A DIVISION OF THOMAS NELSON
& ZONDERVAN

Copyright © 2014 Christa Erario.

All rights reserved. No part of this book may be used or reproduced by any means, graphic, electronic, or mechanical, including photocopying, recording, taping or by any information storage retrieval system without the written permission of the publisher except in the case of brief quotations embodied in critical articles and reviews.

Scripture taken from the King James Version of the Bible.

Scripture quotations marked (GNT) are from the Good News Translation in Today's English Version —-Second Edition. Copyright 1992 by American Bible Society. Used by permission.

Scripture texts in this work marked NAB are taken from the *New American Bible, revised edition 2010, 1991, 1986,* 1970. Confraternity of Christian Doctrine, Washington, DC, and are used by permission of copyright owner. All rights reserved. No part of the New American Bible may be reproduced in any form without permission from the copyright owner.

Drawings marked A, B, C, D, and E are used by permission of the copyright owner, artist Jean Keaton (www.jeankeatonart.com). All rights reserved.

Drawings marked 1 through 9 are used by permission of the artist, Marie Chombok, and her son, Ernest Chombok.

WestBow Press books may be ordered through booksellers or by contacting:

WestBow Press
A Division of Thomas Nelson & Zondervan
1663 Liberty Drive
Bloomington, IN 47403
www.westbowpress.com
1 (866) 928-1240

Because of the dynamic nature of the Internet, any web addresses or links contained in this book may have changed since publication and may no longer be valid. The views expressed in this work are solely those of the author and do not necessarily reflect the views of the publisher, and the publisher hereby disclaims any responsibility for them.

Any people depicted in stock imagery provided by Thinkstock are models, and such images are being used for illustrative purposes only.
Certain stock imagery © Thinkstock.

ISBN: 978-1-4908-5107-5 (sc)
ISBN: 978-1-4908-5109-9 (hc)
ISBN: 978-1-4908-5108-2 (e)

Library of Congress Control Number: 2014915948

Printed in the United States of America.

WestBow Press rev. date: 11/7/2014

Dedicated to Don, who gave me
forty-four years of his love,
through good times and bad.

Contents

Part 1: God's Great Loving Care and Protection for us 1

Isaiah 49:15, 16 (NAB) 5
Matthew 28:20 (NAB) 7
Mark 15:34 (GNT) 9
Baruch 5:9 (GNT) 10
Isaiah 54:10 (GNT) 13
1 Corinthian 1:24, 25 (NAB) 14
Psalm 30:12, 13 (NAB) 15
Psalm 28:7 (GNT) 16
John 16:23, 24 (NAB) 17
2 Timothy 1:7 (KJV) 19
Jeremiah 1:9, 10 (GNT) 20
Romans 11:36 (NAB) 21
Zechariah 9:16, 17 (GNT) 23
Matthew 26:10, 11 (NAB) 24
John 15:9, 10 (GNT) 25
Mark 16:3, 4 (GNT) 26
Ezekiel 3:24 (NAB) 27
Isaiah 9:1 (NAB) 29
Hebrews 12:12, 13 (GNT) 30
Jeremiah 39:17, 18 (GNT) 31
Jonah 2:7 (GNT) 32

Zechariah 10:11, 12 (GNT) 33
Zephaniah 3:17 (GNT) 34
Psalm 131 (NAB) 35
Letter of Jeremiah 5–7 (GNT) 36
Song of Songs 1:4 (GNT) 37
Esther 2:16, 17 (GNT) 38
2 Esdras 7:49 (GNT) 39
Isaiah 26:3, 4 (NAB) 40
2 Corinthians 4:18 (NAB) 41
1 Esdras 7:15 (GNT) 42
Mark 8:31 (GNT) 43
Jeremiah 46:27 (GNT) 44
Amos 5:8 (NAB) 45
Matthew 5:48 (NAB) 46
2 Maccabees 8:18, 19 (GNT) 47
Jeremiah 52:32–34 (GNT) 50
1 Esdras 8:74–76 (GNT) 51

Part 2: God's Own Beloved Children 53

Wisdom of Solomon 7:15, 16 (GNT) 57
1 John 3:1 (GNT) 59
Hosea 13:4 (NAB) 60
1 Maccabees 7:18 (NAB) 61
Romans 12:12, 13 (GNT) 62
Esther 10:6, 7 (GNT) 63
Esther 9:1, 2 (GNT) 64

Psalm 127:2 (GNT)	65
John 21:5, 6 (NAB)	66
1 Maccabees 6:8 (GNT)	67
Wisdom 15:1, 2 (NAB)	68
Song of the Three Young Men 66, 67 (GNT)	69
Luke 17:5, 6 (NAB)	70
Wisdom 9:17, 18 (GNT)	71
Daniel 9:17–19 (GNT)	72
Sirach 10:28, 29 (GNT)	73
John 1:1 (NAB)	74
Mark 6:49–51 (GNT)	75
Matthew 11:28–30 (NAB)	76
Psalm 122:3 (GNT)	77
Isaiah 53:5, 6 (NAB)	78
2 Corinthians 5:17 (NAB)	79
Jonah 2:6 (NAB)	80
Amos 9; 11 (GNT)	81
Ezekiel 16:8–10, 14 (NAB)	82
Habakkuk 2:14 (NAB)	83
John 8:28, 29 (NAB)	84
Acts 9:3–5 (NAB)	85
Psalm 111:7–9 (NAB)	86
Matthew 22:44 (NAB)	87
Luke 1:52 (NAB)	88
Ecclesiastes 9:9 (NAB)	89
John 2:10 (NAB)	90

John 3:16 (NAB) 93

John 1:12, 13 (NAB) 94

Isaiah 58:10 (NAB) 95

Mark 7:14, 15 (NAB) 96

Haggai 2:7, 8 (NAB) 97

John 3:31–33 (NAB) 98

Luke 1:76 (NAB) 99

Jeremiah 38:20 (NAB) 100

John 1:14 (NAB) 101

1 Maccabees 5:29 (NAB) 102

Jeremiah 10:12, 13 (GNT) 103

Wisdom 15:3 (NAB) 104

Wisdom 9:2–4 (NAB) 105

Tobit 13:10 (GNT) 106

Sirach 33:20 (GNT). 107

Matthew 10:40 (GNT) 108

Matthew 20:16 (NAB) 109

Psalm 127:1 (GNT) 110

Jonah 2:9 (GNT) 111

Part 3: Love, the Greatest Commandment 113

1 Corinthians 13:4–6 (NAB) 117

Mark 12:30, 31 (NAB) 118

Matthew 22:37, 38 (NAB) 119

Mark 8:34 (NAB) 123

1 John 4:18 (KJV) 124

Mark 8:35 (NAB) 125
Mark 8:36, 37 (KJV) 126
Mark 8:38 (NAB) 127
John 8:31, 32 (NAB) 128
Mark 12:30 ... all your heart (NAB) 129
Mark 12:30 ... all your soul (NAB) 130
Mark 12:30 ... all your mind (NAB) 131
Mark 12:30 ... all your strength (NAB) 132
Matthew 22:39, 40 (NAB) 133

Part 4: Victory in Jesus 135

Matthew 27:37 (NAB) 139
Matthew 18:10 (NAB) 141
Micah 2:12, 13 (NAB) 142
Jeremiah 1:5 (NAB) 143
Acts 13:29, 30 (NAB) 145
Psalm 46:1, 2 (KJV) 146
1 Corinthians 1:4–6 (NAB) 147
Luke 24:36–38 (NAB) 148
Luke 1:52 (NAB) 149
Matthew 14:25, 26 (NAB) 150
Mark 8:15 (GNT) 151
Mark 9:2, 3, 7 (NAB) 152
Matthew 26:36, 38 (NAB) 155
Joel 2:25, 26 (NAB) 156
Acts 19:11, 12 (NAB) 157

Daniel 10:11, 12 (NAB) 158
Ezekiel 28:25, 26 (NAB) 159
Ezekiel 36:26–28 (NAB) 160
Mark 7:26–28 (NAB) 161
Amos 5:6 (NAB) 162
Psalm 115:15, 16, 18 (NAB) 163
Matthew 10:34–36 (NAB) 164
Matthew 6:31–33 (NAB) 165
Ezekiel 37:26, 27 (NAB) 166
Mark 13:31 (NAB) 167
Habakkuk 3:2 (NAB) 168
Jeremiah 46:27, 28 (NAB) 169
Mark 14:24, 25 (NAB) 170
Tobit 12:7 (GNT) 171
Zechariah 1:14–17 (NAB) 172

About the Writer

Christa Erario was born on July 5, 1941, in Berlin, Germany. She emigrated to America with her family in December 1952 and lived in the Queens, New York, area until her marriage in July 1968. At that time, she and her husband moved to Long Island, New York, where they raised three children. She is recently widowed and has one grandchild.

A member of the charismatic prayer group's healing team at Christa's local parish. She is also a past member of an inner healing team on Long Island. It was there that she started writing these *Loves Notes from the Heart of God.* The team was hosting a retreat and the leader of the team asked for volunteers who would pray and ask God for love Scripture quotes and that the Lord would give a word to write with it, for each one of the retreatants. Christa volunteered, and after that, whenever people asked her for a word from the Lord, over several years, she would do the same. After a time, the Lord gave her the name *Love Notes*.

On the Feast of Our Lady of Fatima, 2013

Dear Lord,

Why are your Love Notes to me so very different from the messages at Fatima and at Lourdes?

Because this is the great outpouring of my divine mercy on the world. Because it comes straight from the heart of God, kept there from the creation of the world, original intent.

The world is full of anguish and pain.
Tired are my feet,
but still I press on.
Will no one hear my call?
I knock, but none will answer.

The world is full of strife and pain,
and the people bow their heads in shame;
I long to hold them, love them.
Be my hands and heart, my child.

The world is full of hunger and oppression.
My people cry out with fear.
I call, but no one hears my call.
Be my food and drink, my child.

My people live in sadness and pain;
Their wails and moans reach to the skies.
I long to heal their pain and sorrow,
but no one answers me.
Be my bread and wine, my child.

Part 1

God's Great Loving Care and Protection for us

UNDER THE WINGS

of the Dove,

thou shalt live in peace

and fear will reign no more.

A

I will never forget you. See, upon the palms
of my hands I have written your name.
—Isaiah 49:15, 16 (NAB)

Before the world was made, I knew you. I created you in my image and likeness so that I could love you, care for you, and share my life with you. You are very loved, my child. Believe me in this. It is important that you know this.

B

And know that I am with you always,
even until the end of the age.
—Matthew 28:20 (NAB)

I tell you the truth. I am always here with you, child. You are never alone. I hold you close to my heart; I love you so much. I will never let you go.

> My God, my God! Why have you abandoned me?
> —Mark 15:34 (GNT)

Sometimes, you feel all alone, but I am always right here with you, child. Trust in me to be here for you whenever you need me, and whatever you need me to be for you.

Sometimes you feel all alone, but I am always here with you, child, carrying you through the hardest time. I love you, child. Trust me.

God will lead Israel home. They will return with great joy, guided by his mercy and righteousness, surrounded by the light of his glorious presence.
—Baruch 5:9 (GNT)

I will lead you home to my Father in heaven. My righteousness shall be your shield and my mercy shall envelop you. I love you so much, my child; you cannot fathom it.

C

"The mountains and hills may crumble, but my love for you will never end; I will keep forever my promise of peace." So says the Lord who loves you.
—Isaiah 54:10 (GNT)

You are my child and I will lead to a place of rest in my arms of love. I am always with you, child, to protect and deliver you. Have no fear.

But those who are called, Jews and Greeks alike, Christ the power of God and the wisdom of God. For the foolishness of God is wiser than human wisdom, and the weakness of God is stronger than human strength.
—1 Corinthian 1:24, 25 (NAB)

My power is upon you, child. The greatest power in heaven and on earth is at your disposal if you do my will. It is the power to transform hate into love and compassion, sorrow and pain into joy and jubilation, and discord into peace. All this and more is my gift to you from the cross. This then is my foolishness and my strength.

You changed my mourning into dancing; you took
off my sackcloth and clothed me with gladness, that
my soul might sing praise to you without ceasing.
O Lord, my God, forever will I give you thanks.
—Psalm 30:12, 13 (NAB)

Pray without seeking favor from me. Pure joy in just being with me is when you give me praise. Be with me, and I will truly turn your mourning into dancing. Just the thought of being alive in me will bring you joy. Never fear. Trust in me; I am here with you, dear.

The Lord protects and defends me; I trust in him. He gives me help and makes me glad; I praise him with joyful songs.
—Psalm 28:7 (GNT)

I am your defender, the Paraclete, and I protect you from your enemies who try to come against you. You are my child. I love you so, and I take care of my own. You are safe from harm under my protection, and I will never—I repeat, *never*—leave you or abandon you. This truth held deep in your heart will make you glad. So rejoice.

On that day, you will have no question to ask of me. I give you my assurance, whatever you ask of the Father, he will give to you in my name. Until now you have not asked for anything in my name. Ask and you shall receive, that your joy may be full.
—John 16:23, 24 (NAB)

But first, you must be willing to do and accept my will in all things. For then you will be asking for my will to be done, and I and the Father are one. You will be doing my will, which will help me bless you and others through you. So ask and it will be given to you. In abundance, till it overflows, will you receive that your joy may be in me. Enjoy my abounding, unlimited love.

2

For God has not given us a spirit of fear, but of power and of love and of a sound mind.
—2 Timothy 1:7 (KJV)

Give in to me and do not fear, so that I will be able to lead you where I want to you to be. Gladly will I lead you to the place of rest in my love, where you will be safe from fear. Do not fret about the rest. Just rest in my love, where you will find peace and contentment. What is this "rest" you speak of so much? Be with me and trust in me for everything. And trust that, after surrendering everything to me, I will take care of you and all your petitions; rest in my loving care.

Then the Lord reached out, touched my lips, and said to me, "Listen, I am giving you the words you must speak, Today I give you authority over nations and kingdoms to uproot and pull down, to destroy and to overthrow, to build and to plant."
—Jeremiah 1:9, 10 (GNT)

There is so much here that it will take all day to tell you. But to sum it up, I will give you a little. Do as I say, and you will tear down barriers of long-standing for all times to come. My Word is everlasting.

For from him and through him and for him
all things are. To him be glory forever.
—Romans 11:36 (NAB)

As I am in you, so you are in me. Then you also were made by my hands. You are my handiwork, and as such, you are beautiful. I created you out of love to be my beloved child—beloved of the Father and the Son and the Holy Spirit. You are to be mine through all eternity. Please accept my gift of life. I love you so much.

3

When that day comes, the Lord will save his people, as a shepherd saves a flock from danger. They will shine in his land like the jewels of a crown. How good and beautiful the land will be! The young people will grow strong on its grain and wine.
—Zechariah 9:16, 17 (GNT)

For you are my son, born by my only begotten Son's death on the cross and redeemed by his blood for all eternity to be my own dear child. As such, I will take care of all of your faults and failings and heal all of your hurts. Just give all to me, and trust me to deliver you. I love you, my child. You are very precious to me.

Jesus said to them, "Why do you criticize the woman? It is a good deed she done for me. The poor you will always have with you, but you will not always have me."
—Matthew 26:10, 11 (NAB)

What you have done for me is not lost or stolen. It is a sweet incense reaching up to heaven. I approve of you and all of your work done for love of me. Thank you, my beloved daughter.

I love you just as the Father loves me; remain in my love. If you obey my commands, you will remain in my love, just as I have obeyed my Father's commands and remain in his love.
—John 15:9, 10 (GNT)

I am in you just as the Father is in me. Remaining in my love means to obey what I tell you to do; follow my guidance. Then you will live in my love and I will live in you and through you. Come follow me, my beloved. I love you and want so much to be able to live in you and through you.

On the way, they said to one another, "Who will roll away the stone for us from the entrance of the tomb?" (It was a very big stone.) Then they looked up and saw that the stone had already been rolled back.
—Mark 16:3, 4 (GNT)

You are my child and I will take care of you. Believe me in this, and you will know a life richer and fuller than you ever dreamed of or imagined. It may not be all you wanted it to be. No. It will be far more meaningful and richer. A life more full of my riches from my kingdom, the kingdom of God. Riches only my children can possess. I love you, child. Trust me that I know what is best for you. I have a plan for your life—a very good plan.

But then Spirit entered into me and set me
on my feet, and he spoke with me.
—Ezekiel 3:24 (NAB)

Y ou have my Spirit in you. Know that I am always with you and would speak through you, but you must trust me and know that I am speaking through you. You cannot help me by being afraid. If you are afraid but trust me, my Spirit will lift you up above the fear.

E

The people who walked in darkness have
seen a great light; Upon those who dwell in
the land of gloom a light has shone.
—Isaiah 9:1 (NAB)

My light illumines all the dark places. Let me come into you, shine in all the dark places of your heart, and restore your soul. Your soul is in my hands. My light is shining on your soul, and I hold it close to my heart so that you will always be protected by my love, which is the light that shines in the darkness, and the darkness has never succeeded in putting it out. My child, I am always with you, even in the dark times of your life. Trust in me. I am the Word that is your lamp that lights your way.

Lift up your tired hands, then, and strengthen your trembling knees! Keep walking on straight paths, so that the lame foot may not be disabled, but instead be healed.
—Hebrews 12:12, 13 (GNT)

As you know, I love you and will heal you, and I am already healing you internally (your heart, the core of your being). Wait for my guidance, and then dance an eternal dance with me. Between us, there can't be any false sense of self or lies to create friction. Just the ebb and flow of love to be transferred from one to the other.

But I, the Lord, will protect you, and you will not be handed over to the men you are afraid of. I will keep you safe, and you will not be put to death. You will escape with your life because you have put your trust in me. I, the Lord, have spoken.
—Jeremiah 39:17, 18 (GNT)

What I will do for anyone who calls on me, I will do for you. I am your protector and shield. Trust in me to protect you at every crossing. I am the wall that surrounds you at every angle (above and below too). You can bank (rely) on me to keep you safe from harm of any kind. I love you, dear, and my love is everlasting and unchangeable.

When I felt my life slipping away, then, O Lord, I prayed to you, and in your holy Temple you heard me.
—Jonah 2:7 (GNT)

As long as you come to me with your needs, I will answer them. I have the answer already prepared with tender, loving care and await your call. You are very precious to me, and I take care of my beloved children when they call on me. I wait for their call with an impatience only few can understand. I love you, my child.

When they pass through their sea of trouble, I, the Lord will strike the waves and the depths of the Nile will go dry. Proud Assyria will be humbled, and mighty Egypt will lose her power. I will make my people strong. They will worship and obey me." The Lord has spoken.
—Zechariah 10:11, 12 (GNT)

I am the Lord, your God. I will make all things possible if you trust in me. That is the prerequisite for getting my help. When you trust me, I will act powerfully on your behalf and open the door for your help to come through. I will do this; just trust me. Believe in my care for you.

The Lord, your God, is with you; his power
gives you victory. The Lord will take delight in
you, and in his love will give you new life.
—Zephaniah 3:17 (GNT)

I am with you, child. Please me and give your worries to me. As you are near me in prayer, in a strange and wonderful way, I am preparing great things for you by means of my love. Behold, I am your God, the Almighty, and I will do great things for you. My Word is your key to my kingdom of love, joy, and peace. Be calm, my friend. Peace be to you.

Lord, my heart is not proud; nor my eyes haughty. I do not busy myself with great matters, with things too sublime for me. Rather, I have stilled my soul, hushed it like a weaned child. Like a weaned child on it mother's lap, so is my soul within me. Israel, hope in the Lord, now and forever.
—Psalm 131 (NAB)

This is my promise to you, if you will trust in me: your quiet times will turn into peace and contentment in my arms of love. Let everything else go. Just sit and trust in my power to complete everything with my love and wisdom. I love you so-o much that I will take care of all of your needs, if you trust them to me. I am all you will ever need.

Don't let their gods fill you with fear when you see them being carried in procession and being worshiped. Instead, say to yourselves, "It is you alone, Lord, that we must worship." God's angel will be there with you; he will take care of you.
—Letter of Jeremiah 5–7 (GNT)

I am the Lord, your God, the Almighty, all-powerful God. You are my child, born of my Word on the cross. Be careful then to act in response to my love for you, a deep and abiding love that is deeper than anything you can imagine. It is this love that flows from me to you and then back to me again through others that you share my love with.

Take me with you and we'll run away; be my king and take me to your room. We will be happy together, drink deep, and lose ourselves in love.
—Song of Songs 1:4 (GNT)

As I am in you, so you are in me. As I live in you, you are my instrument for my work on earth to be done. As you move, I move also. But for this to happen, you have to come to me first, your beloved, and spend time with me. Come away with me in the silence of our hearts until our hearts beat as one.

Esther was brought to king Xerxes in the royal palace. The king liked her more than any of the other girls, and more than any of the others she won his favor and affection. He placed a royal crown on her head and made her queen in place of Vashti.
—Esther 2:16, 17 (GNT)

You are my child—a queen, of sorts, because I favor you with my graces to keep you close to me in times of trials. You are so precious to me that I do not allow anyone else to favor you with any graces or blessings. You are my queen in captivity because I allow no one rights over you. I want you all to myself. I love you so much, my daughter.

"Listen to me," the angel said, "and I will teach you further and correct your thinking."
—2 Esdras 7:49 (GNT)

I am your Father, the Almighty, eternal God. I will teach you everything you need to know to do my will for you in your life. I will give you the opportunities to realize those goals. Just be open to my inspiration and guidance. My will for your life is for you to be at peace and to trust me to lead, guide, and help you in all circumstances. No matter what, believe and know that I am in charge.

A nation firm in purpose you will keep in peace;
in peace, for its trust in you. Trust in the Lord
forever! For the Lord is an eternal rock.
—Isaiah 26:3, 4 (NAB)

I am your Lord, God Almighty, your Savior and your shield for all times to come. I am your father, mother, and guide, controller of your destiny and guide and shepherd into eternity. Think more on me, your God and lover, than on anything or anyone else. I and my will should come first in your life. Then everything else will fall into place. I love you, child. Do my will; it pleases me to no end.

We do not fix our gaze on what is seen but on what is unseen. What is seen is transitory; what is unseen lasts forever.
—2 Corinthians 4:18 (NAB)

This is heaven, to know me and the one who sent me. To really know me, you must let go of everything that hinders you from getting to know me, your Lord and Savior, and my Father and the Holy Spirit, who I will send to you to enlighten you regarding heavenly truths. I will teach you about the unseen world, the eternal wisdom of the ages. Don't be concerned about this world's concerns, but be conformed to eternal truths by the Holy Spirit's power. I love you so, child. Be at peace. I am here with you in a foreign land. Foreign to you because you are with me, the great foreigner.

They rejoiced in the presence of the Lord, the God of Israel, because he had made the plans of the emperor of Assyria favorable to them and had supported them in their work.
—1 Esdras 7:15 (GNT)

I am with you always, your Father, your God, your leader out of difficulties. Always lean and rely on me to be your support, not only in times of trial but always. All support, whether physical, mental, or emotional, comes from me, your God and provider of all that you will ever need. I am with you and for you always. Believe me in this, please, my precious child. I love you so much.

Then Jesus began to teach his disciples: "The Son of Man must suffer much and be rejected by the elders, the chief priests, and the teachers of the law. He will be put to death, but three days later he will rise to life. He made this very clear to them."
—Mark 8:31 (GNT)

I am the resurrection and the life. He who comes to me is a changed person. You cannot be with me and not be changed. I change you into a new person, one who responds to my love and life happily with love. You are my person of delight because I lay claim on you and I perform all of your needs to my satisfaction. And that means protecting you from harm of any kind. Have no fear, but look forward to a life lived with me, your protector. Be happy, child, and look forward to life's surprises in your new life. I am always with you, dear.

My people do not be afraid, people of Israel; do not be terrified. I will rescue you from that faraway land where you are prisoners. You will come back home and live in peace; you will be secure, and no one will make you afraid. I will come to you and save you.
—Jeremiah 46:27 (GNT)

Do as I say, and you will again be whole. As parched earth needs and yearns for water, so I will quench your need and yearning to be whole. I will do this if you will be open to my healing touch, my inspiration, and my guidance. But first, you have to let go of everything that hinders you from following me and my will for your life. Come follow me, my beloved, and we will walk together through life into eternity.

He who made the Pleiades and Orion, who turns darkness into dawn, and darkens day into night; who summons the waters of the sea, and pours them out upon the surface of the earth.
—Amos 5:8 (NAB)

As you are in me, so I am in you as your brother, friend, and guide through life. I am always with you. Do not fear or fret, for I am directing and guiding you to greater heights. Come into me and let me love you and make you whole and well. How do I come into you, Lord? Accept what is, and I will do the rest. Rest in my loving care, and I will take care of everything.

> You must be perfect—just as your
> heavenly Father is perfect.
> —Matthew 5:48 (NAB)

You are my child, and that means you are perfect, for every one that is born again of water and the Holy Spirit is perfect because I died for them on the cross. You were made perfect by my sacrifice. The material is only illusion that can be brought low. Like my death on the cross was followed by my resurrection, so you will have your resurrection moment.

"They rely on their weapons and daring," Judas said, "but we trust in Almighty God, who is able to destroy not only these troops, but, if necessary, this entire world with a mere nod off his head." Then Judas went on to remind them of the ways God had helped their ancestors.
—2 Maccabees 8:18, 19 (GNT)

There is a little-known fact that I want to reveal to you today about this story, which is that I orchestrated everything that happened including healing their sick as they came to me. I am the destroyer, but I am also the healer of all of your wounds—every one of them. I wish to make you whole, spiritually and physically. You are my child; I am your parent—father, mother, brother, companion, and guide. I love you, child. Believe that I am here with you always.

(2 Maccabees 8:18, 19) - 2 –

This is the way I work. Trust in me, and I will help you in whatever your need is. I will act powerfully on your behalf and open doors you cannot open for yourself. I am your healer, father, mother, brother, companion, and guide. I love you, child. Trust and rely on me to be there for you for everything. I am always with you, dear.

(2 Maccabees 8:18, 19) - 3 –

As I said before, this is my way, my plan for dealing with life's hurts and circumstances.

First, you will trust in my goodness and loving care of and for you.

Second, you will bring me honor by believing in my Word (the Holy Bible), the words I speak to you privately, after having them confirmed.

And third, follow the guidance of the Holy Spirit within you. These are my commandments to you, child. You will be pleased with the results, if you obey them. Never fail to trust in my loving care for you. It is always there, ready at any moment to lend a hand, to heal, or to clear the way for you to travel down life's road to me and with me your God and Savior.

Evil-merodach treated him kindly and gave him a position of greater honor than he gave his other kings who were in exile with him in Babylonia. So Jehoiachin was permitted to change from his prison clothes and to dine at the king's table for the rest of his life. Each day for as long as he lived, he was given a regular allowance for his needs.
—Jeremiah 52:32–34 (GNT)

As you know, I am always with you, loving you and providing for you, giving you my wisdom and guidance no matter what is going on around you. I am your refuge in the center of the storm. I will provide for all of your needs to be met, most of all your need for me and my love. I love you, dear. Never fear. I am here, putting everything in my divine order and harmony.

I said, "O Lord, I am ashamed and confused in your presence. Our sins tower over our heads; they reach as high as the heavens. This has been true from the days of our ancestors until now; we, your people, have sinned greatly."
—1 Esdras 8:74–76 (GNT)

I am your God, the Almighty, all-powerful Savior. I bring peace and a wonderful feeling of contentment to your mind and heart. This is my will that you obey and worship only me, your Lord and Savior, the one who saves you from your iniquities. Be at peace, my child. I am with you through it all.

Part 2

God's Own Beloved Children

THE PASSION

of my Savior

is like a perfect melody,

each note sung anew each day

in the recesses of my heart.

I pray to God that my thoughts may be worthy of what I have learned, and that I may speak according to his will. He is Wisdom's guide; he gives correction to those who are wise. We are under his power and authority—we ourselves, our words, all our understanding and skills.
—Wisdom of Solomon 7:15, 16 (GNT)

I am your Lord and Savior of all of your being, of all you possess. Give me your permission to be that for you. I am your Lord and Savior, but more importantly, your king and ruler over all. I am your inheritance. Live with me, my beloved, and I will instruct you in the ways of wisdom. All you are, and all you have—everything comes from me, your God and king.

4

See how much the Father loved us! His love is so great that we are called God's children—and so, in fact, we are. This is why the world does not know us; it has not known God.
—1 John 3:1 (GNT)

I am your Father, the great Father of all created beings and all that is seen and unseen. I created you and all out of love. You were born in love. Whether your earthly parents loved you or not has no bearing on my love for you or your standing in my family. You were born into my family by my Son's death on the cross. You are mine forever. No taking back my Word, my Son. I gave him to you freely, with only one condition that you believe in him. You are loved for all eternity, and no one can take that away from you.

I am the Lord, your God, since the land
of Egypt; You know no god besides me,
and there is no other Savior but me.
—Hosea 13:4 (NAB)

I am your Lord and Savior. The only one who saves from destruction of any kind. You are mine. Mine because I saved you from the enemy, the evil one. I saved you by dying on the cross for you, taking all of your sins and failures upon myself. I made myself responsible for you and all of your sins. By means of this, you are my child again. Now you belong to me only. The devil has no hold on you whatsoever if you come to me for help, which I will gladly give. You are mine. I love you and will take care of you. No one else will.

Then fear and dread of them came over all the people, who said: "There is no truth or justice among them; they violated the agreement and the oath that they swore."
—1 Maccabees 7:18 (NAB)

I am your God, the god of truth and wisdom. I lead you to me by means of the truth. If you don't know the truth, you don't know me. Therefore, I want you to tell them the truth, so they can at least have a change of heart if they want to do right. See me in them, so that you can see that they are pleasing to me. See not the sin but the God who created them in them. Then I feel like crying, Lord, because it is so sad to see them like this, in their sins, knowing they are your children and they don't know it or don't understand what it means. See my dilemma? That is why I need you to tell them and show them the truth about me and my ways. Remember I am the way, the truth, and the life.

Let hope keep you joyful, be patient in your troubles, and pray at all times. Share your belongings with your needy fellow Christians, and open your doors to strangers.
—Romans 12:12, 13 (GNT)

Do for me what I would do for you. I love you, son. You needn't fear to obey me, your God and healer of all of your cares and troubles. You are my child, whether you realize it or not. I will take care of all of your needs. Do not accept fear, for I am always with you and for you. Yes, I said I am for you no matter what you may have done, or didn't do. I am always here for you. You have only to ask for my help, and help will be given. Accept my answer. It may not always be what you expected, but I guarantee it will be better than your petition. I love you, son. Have no fear; I am always with you, dear.

My nation is Israel, which cried out to God for help and was saved. The Lord saved his people! He rescued us from all these evils and performed great miracles and wonders that have never happened among other nations. That is because God prepared one destiny for his own people and another for all other nations.
—Esther 10:6, 7 (GNT)

As I welcome you to my table, you will be welcomed anywhere in the world. You are my child. I will take care of you and all of your illnesses. You belong to me, and as such, you will be forgiven of all of your sins and failings. I am always here with you, child. Believe me in this. Trust in me no matter what outward appearances may say. I will rescue you from evil. Believe it.

The day on which the royal proclamation was to take effect, it was the enemy of the Jews who were wiped out. People everywhere were afraid of the Jews and no one could stand against them.
—Esther 9:1, 2 (GNT)

As I am in you, so you are in me, and as such, you are protected. No evil can befall you or destroy you, no matter what appearances say. You are mine. I will rescue you and restore you to wholeness. You are mine; never forget that for a moment. Trust in me always. I love you so much, my child.

It is useless to work so hard for a living, getting up early and going to bed late. For the Lord provides for those he loves, while they are asleep.
—Psalm 127:2 (GNT)

You are my beloved child. When I created you, I decided to take care of you and supply all of your needs and the plan I had for your life for all eternity. I will provide for all of your needs, even to the smallest details, as long as you put me first and recognize that I am your source of all that is good. I will give you an abundance you cannot conceive and the wisdom to handle it. I will prosper you in every area of your life so that it will amaze you. You are mine, and I am your Father. I am proud of my children, and I like to show them off.

Jesus said to them, "Children have you caught anything to eat?" "Not a thing," they answered. "Cast your nets off to the starboard side," He suggested, "and you will find something." So they made a cast and took in so many fish they could not haul the net in.
—John 21:5, 6 (NAB)

As you obey me, I will fill your life with good things from my storehouse of blessings so abundant you cannot conceive it. I will be your master, guide, friend, and consoler through every difficulty and always. Though at times it may get tough, I will always be there for you to help and console. You will never lack for anything you need. Just trust in me completely. I will always be here for you. I love you, my precious children. I bless you always.

When the king heard this report, he was so dumbfounded and terribly shaken that he went to bed in a fit of deep depression because things had not turned out as he had hoped.
—1 Maccabees 6:8 (GNT)

Because you love me, I will accept your prayer of penance and heal your heart of stone. You are very precious, child. I love you so much that I can hardly stand by to see you suffer so, but I must wait until you are ready to trust that I am here with you and for you. Trust that I will be here for you in each and every need, and that I will be your comforter and help in every difficulty. Trust is my command to you, child.

But you, our God, are good and true, slow to
anger, and governing all with mercy. For even if
we sin, we are yours, and know your might; but we
will not sin, knowing that we belong to you.
—Wisdom 15:1, 2 (NAB)

If you are my child, then I am your Father and I rule with mercy and justice. You are my child if you believe in the truth of my being, a God who longs to love and take care of his children and share his life with them rather than the world's conception of me as a God who sits idly by and watches everything from a window in heaven. I am in all things and all peoples, but I am limited by my creatures because of their free will. I do not impose myself on anyone. They must choose me or the world. Unless people come to me, I cannot help them in their need, and my help far outweighs their need for me, which is so-o great. Believe me in this, and I will open heaven's portals to you and pour out my blessings on you, my precious child.

Praise the Lord; Hananiah, Azariah, and Mishael, sing his praise and honor him forever. He has rescued us from the world of the dead and saved us from the power of death. He brought us out from the burning furnace and saved us from the fire. Give thanks to the Lord for he is good and his mercy lasts forever.
—Song of the Three Young Men 66, 67 (GNT)

As you are in me, so I am in you, and you are my instrument here on earth with which I do my work of deliverance. I am your God, the one who saves and delivers from all sin and death by means of my love and power to heal and strengthen. Do not fear, but remember I am with you through it all, delivering and healing and strengthening.

And the apostles said to the Lord, "Increase our faith" The Lord replied, "If you have faith the size of a mustard seed, you would say to (this) mulberry tree, 'Be uprooted and planted in the sea', and it would obey you."
—Luke 17:5, 6 (NAB)

As from me a flower grows, so do you. I am your Lord, the Almighty. I am with you through it all, so do not fear. You are being led by me if you spend time with me first in the silence of our hearts. Do not forget that. When I call you to spend a little time with me before doing a certain task I told you to do, come and spend that time with me. It will be well worth the effort it takes to stop what you are doing for a short while. Everything will go smoother and better than you anticipated, and we can get much greater things accomplished.

No one has ever learned your will, unless you first
gave him Wisdom, and sent your holy spirit down
to him. In this way people on earth have been
set on the right path, have learned what pleases
you, and have been kept safe by Wisdom.
—Wisdom 9:17, 18 (GNT)

When you live in me, your Creator, you live in a universe of love and wisdom. Then you are being led by the Spirit of God, who is wisdom itself. You are my beloved child in whom I am well pleased because you are in Christ Jesus, my Son, who is my love incarnate. So do not fear, but remember that I am with you at all times, leading and guiding you in love and wisdom.

O God, hear my prayer and pleading. Restore your temple which has been destroyed; restore it so that everyone will know that you are God. Listen to us o God; look at us and see the trouble we are in and the suffering of the city that bears your name. We are praying to you because you are merciful, not because we have done right. Lord, hear us. Lord, forgive us. Lord, listen to us and act! In order that everyone will know that you are God. Do not delay! This city and these people are yours.
—Daniel 9:17–19 (GNT)

As you rely on me to be your healer and helper out of difficulties, you are being led by my Holy Spirit to guide you into the truth of your being, which is that I am in you and you are in me. Think about that. The God of the universe is in you; then all of the healing power of the universe is also in you. To release this healing power, you have to believe in it. Know it is there within you, acting for you on your behalf. As you relax and let God's love flow through you, rest in my love, you are being healed and restored, and God's healing power is acting in you.

Son keep your self-respect, but remain modest. Value yourself at your true worth. There is no excuse for a person to run himself down. No one respects a person who has no respect for himself.
—Sirach 10:28, 29 (GNT)

As for me and my house, we will worship the Lord our God and only him. This used to be the saying of my people here on earth, but now it has gotten so intermingled with the god of this world saying to worship him too that it is no longer said or the meaning has been so distorted that it no longer means the same thing. You are my child, whether you acknowledge me or not. You are still my child, bought back by the death of my firstborn son, Jesus, on the cross. Therefore, you have dignity and righteousness (right standing with me, your God and Father of all beings). I love you, child, not as an earthly father would but unconditionally and always with tender love and mercy. You are my child and I am proud of you. Love me by loving and respecting yourself. You deserve respect. You are my child.

In the beginning was the Word, and the Word
was with God, and the Word was God.
—John 1:1 (NAB)

I am in you and you are my child. Therefore, I created you out of my love for you. You are my product of love. Love produces more love as well as more of the same. You are produced from my loins. You are a tiny part, seed, of me. I produced you of my own free will so that I may share my life with you and care for you. I enjoy giving you my life to no end because you are my creation. I love you, child, forever.

But they saw him walking on the water. "It's a ghost!" they thought, and screamed. They were all terrified when they saw him. Jesus spoke to them at once, "Courage!" he said. "It is I. Don't be afraid!" Then he got into the boat with them, and the wind died down. The disciples were completely amazed.
—Mark 6:49–51 (GNT)

I am your God, the Almighty, shield from every storm or disaster. Feeder of the hungry of heart and your merciful Savior of all who will accept me. "Be not afraid" was my word to my disciples, and it is my word of encouragement to you too. I am always with you to calm the raging sea inside your mind and to help you through every step of the way of your life. I love you, child. You are mine. Always count on me to be there for you, no matter what, to help, guide, deliver, and protect. I am your Father, the all-knowing, all-wise, all-loving Father forever.

Come to me, all you who labor and are burdened,
and I will give you rest. Take my yoke upon you
and learn from me, for I am meek and humble
of heart, and you will find rest for yourselves.
For my yoke is easy, and my burden is light.
—Matthew 11:28–30 (NAB)

I am your God, the Almighty, all-powerful God. Give all of your burdens to me, your burden bearer, and take up the cross I give you, which is nothing more than believing in my loving care for you and my wisdom and readiness to help you in any and all circumstances. I am your help in every need, no matter what it is, if you follow the guidance of the Holy Spirit. I love you unconditionally. Really knowing that I am here for you constantly makes your life easier to bear, and you can rest in my loving care.

> Jerusalem is a city restored in
> beautiful order and harmony.
> —Psalm 122:3 (GNT)

In my knowledge, there is wisdom and understanding. Pray for my knowledge to understand my world of order and harmony. Then you can understand my thinking a little more clearly. I am order and harmony. If you are in me, my order is transferred to you by means of my understanding and guidance by my Holy Spirit, the comforter. As you realize more and more that I live in you and you in me, your life will become more orderly and peaceful until peace and joy become the overriding factors in your life. Know that I am here with you all the time, loving and guiding you and putting everything in divine order and harmony, restoring your being and your world.

But he was pierced for our offenses, crushed for our sins. Upon him was the chastisement that makes us whole, by his stripes we were healed. We had all gone astray like sheep, each following his own way, but the Lord laid upon him the guilt of us all.
—Isaiah 53:5, 6 (NAB)

I am your God, the Almighty, all-powerful God of the universe who created everything by his hands, and I created you too to be my very own child for all eternity. I knew that you would fall into sin without me, so I sent my Son, my Word, to deliver you from sin and death and to cleanse you from all that is not of me, all deceptions and lies that you accumulated in your short life here on earth. Accept my will for you and please me by spending more time with me. You are my child, and as you trust in me and rely on me more and more, I will protect you from all evil. I promise, and I always keep my promises. I never fail.

So whoever is in Christ he is a new creation: the old things have passed away; behold, new things have come.
—2 Corinthians 5:17 (NAB)

I am in you just as you are in me. The natural world believes only what it can see with its' eyes, but in the spiritual world, what is unseen is more real than the natural world. Thus, you being in me means relying on me for everything, even the very air you breathe, because it is my Spirit that you are breathing in. Trust and rely on me to be there for you at every moment. Nothing but the best for my children.

The waters swirled about me, threatening my life; the
abyss enveloped me; seaweed clung about my head.
—Jonah 2:6 (NAB)

I will rescue you too from your dire circumstance. Be glad in me. Trust me to be there for you. I am your healer and guide into health and wholeness for body and soul. Remember "I restore your soul" (Psalm 23). I am your healer and guide into eternity. I am with you always. Hope and trust in me to be there for you. I love you so.

The Lord says, "A day is coming when I will restore the kingdom of David, which is like a house fallen into ruins. I will repair its walls and restore it. I will rebuild it and make it as it was long ago."
—Amos 9; 11 (GNT)

Do not fear anything, as I am with you, as I promised long ago, I would be with my people in their need, and I do not change. I am your God, the Almighty, all-powerful God. I will restore you to health and wholeness, as you trust in me to do it. That is my requirement: trust in my goodness and willingness to help and forgive all of your sins and failings. Yes, I am first and foremost a God of mercy and love. Believe in me. I am with you and for you always. I love you so, my child.

Again I passed by you and saw that you were now old enough for love; so I spread the corner of my cloak over you to cover your nakedness; I swore an oath to you and entered into a covenant with you; you became mine, says the Lord God. Then I bathed you with water, washed away your blood, and anointed you with oil. I clothed you with an embroidered gown, put sandals of fine leather on your feet; I gave you a fine linen sash and a silk robe to wear … my splendor which I had bestowed on you, says the Lord God.
—Ezekiel 16:8–10, 14 (NAB)

I am the all-powerful, Almighty, omnipotent God. Trust in me to deliver you from all evil. Even sickness and disease hold no power over me, nor does heartbreak or sin. All will fall away at my command. My children are mine to command and enjoy. Glory to the Lord, the God of Abraham and Isaac. Here is my command to you: trust and do not doubt my love for you or willingness to heal and make whole. Remember I am Life.

But the earth shall be filled with the knowledge
of the Lord's glory as water covers the sea.
—Habakkuk 2:14 (NAB)

As I am in you so, naturally, the Holy Spirit is in you also, and so the Father too. We are all glorified in you as you let us lead you and act through you. The Holy Spirit helps you to establish a line of communication between you and God. This is very necessary for your well-being and for others'. In so doing, you are acting in cooperation with the Holy Spirit and thus the Holy Trinity. Because you need this guidance, it is provided for you by us in unison with your prayer and by surrendering your will to our will. We love you dearly. Be at peace; we are with you always.

Jesus continued: "When you lift up the Son of Man you will come to realize that I Am and that I do nothing by myself. I say only what the Father has taught me. The one who sent me is with me. He has not deserted me since I always do what pleases him."
—John 8:28, 29 (NAB)

John was my disciple just as you are my disciple. You do my work when you listen to me. I will make you understand many things that you are unable to understand in the natural realm. My Father's will will be done when you listen to the guidance of the Holy Spirit and do what he tells you to do. We are all one: the Father, Son, and Holy Spirit. Do what we tell you to do, and you too will glorify us. We love you, and we want the best life possible for you.

On his journey, as he was nearing Damascus, a light from the sky suddenly flashed around him. He fell to the ground and heard a voice saying to him "Saul, Saul, why do you persecute me?" He said, "Who are you, sir?" The reply came, "I am Jesus, whom you are persecuting."
—Acts 9:3–5 (NAB)

Why are you doubting me? I am here within you and around you, so why all the doubt about everything? I am your Jesus, God of the universe. I am here just for you. I lived and died to take away your sins and make a new and everlasting covenant with you. My faithfulness is your reward from my merciful heart. I say to you, as I said to my doubting friend Thomas, don't doubt any longer but believe that I took all of your sins on the cross and washed them away with my own blood. I rose to new life as you will rise to new life, innocent and blameless before the Father as you repent of your sins. I love you, my brother. Be at peace.

The works of your hands are right and true;
reliable all your decrees, established forever and
ever to be observed with loyalty and care. You sent
deliverance to your people, ratified your covenant
forever; holy and awesome is your name.
—Psalm 111:7–9 (NAB)

I am the God of Israel, but I am your God too. I wield my scepter with love and mercy for all my children, but I am a God of vengeance to all who hate me. I am here with you always to protect, deliver, and guide you through all of life's ups and downs into a place of victory, peace, and contentment. Just follow my guidance; I will lead you, my precious child. Accept my peace.

The Lord said to my Lord, "Sit at my right hand
until I place your enemies under your feet."
—Matthew 22:44 (NAB)

I am your Lord and Savior, the Messiah, the Anointed One. I will do for you what I do for anyone who calls on me. I will help you through every doubt to rest in my loving care. Yes, I will help you and care for you. I care deeply about you. You are the joy of my heart, precious child.

He has thrown down the rulers from their thrones but lifted up the lowly.
—Luke 1:52 (NAB)

I am the God that rules the firmament, the stars. The whole universe I laid out from the beginning of creation so that I could share my life with that of my creatures, who we made in our image and likeness. I made them a home on this planet with everything they needed for all time. I am a God full of love and mercy. I search the earth knocking on every heart for entrance. Those who reject me are lost to me, which causes me great pain, but those who receive me rejoice with me in my love and mercy. I knock on your heart's door this Christmas. Will you bid me, the God of the universe, the infant Jesus, the Savior of the world, your redemption, come in? I love you so. You are very precious, my child.

Enjoy life with the wife whom you love, all the days of the fleeting life that is granted you under the sun.
—Ecclesiastes 9:9 (NAB)

I invite you to new life in me, your God and king over all beings and all creation. I am your Bridegroom; you are my bride, so to speak. Live in me, and I will live in you now and for all eternity. Will you accept my gift of life? The choice is yours, my friend. I love you for all eternity and will not abandon you. Please do not reject me.

The headwaiter called the bridegroom and said to him, "Everyone serves the good wine first, and then when people have drunk freely, an inferior one; but you have kept the good wine until now."
—John 2:10 (NAB)

As you are near me in prayer, I forge a new way for your life. At that instant, your life is changed from drab (dung heap) to crystal-clear water of life; life eternal I give to you. Your life is changed forever to be with me, your Lord and Savior and friend for all times. Believe that I am with you always, your friend, guide, and compassionate healer. Remember I am health and wholeness; I am the essence of life, your loving, merciful God. I bring you hope and healing of body and soul. I love you, child. You are mine forever, if you so wish. Come closer to me. My arms are always open, waiting for you.

5

SIC DEUS DILEXIT MUNDUM

John 3:16

For God so loved the world that He gave His only Son, so that everyone who believes in Him might not perish but have eternal life.
—John 3:16 (NAB)

I am the resurrection and the life. He who accepts me accepts my *LIFE*-giving power to claim the kingdom of God within them through my work on the cross of Calvary. I am a God who claimed all of earth's creatures back to me from the evil one. That is my intent and purpose for everyone who accepts me, and it shall be so. Amen.

But to those who did accept him he gave the power to become children of God, to those who believe in his name, who were born not by natural generation nor by human choice, nor by man's decision but of God.
—John 1:12, 13 (NAB)

I am the God of the universe and all that is seen and unseen. I am here within you. The Holy Trinity is within you. Can you fathom that? Like a seed grows out of the ground nourished by sun and water, so my power of love and truth blooms within you. By telling you this, you are noticing me more and more inside you. I am the God of the universe, yet I make my home in my creatures whom I love beyond your ken. Believe me in this, my precious child.

If you bestow your bread on the hungry and satisfy the afflicted, then light shall rise for you in the darkness, and the gloom shall become for you like midday.
—Isaiah 58:10 (NAB)

As I am in you, you are being formed into my image more and more so that my will can be done in you and through you. My will for you is that you rest in my arms of love and peace. Then I can heal you and provide everything you will need for your life for you and others through you. But you have to trust in my goodness and care for you. You have to expect and rely on me for everything. I love you, child; trust me.

Jesus summoned the crowd again and said to them: "Hear me all of you and understand. Nothing that enters one from outside can defile that person, but the things that come out from within are what defile."
—Mark 7:14, 15 (NAB)

As I am in you, no connection with me and my enemy is possible. Yours is the kingdom of God, if you so wish it to be. Yours is all I have if you count everything else as nothing compared to me, your Lord and Master. There has been so much dissent and strife over my being in you. You are lacking nothing, be it spiritual or physical. No one can make you defiled except your own belief of yourself, of what you truly are. The truth is you are my beloved child, and no one can take that away from you.

"I will shake the nations, and the treasures of the nations will come in. And I will fill this house with glory," says the Lord of Hosts. "Mine is the silver and mine is the gold," says the Lord of Hosts.
—Haggai 2:7, 8 (NAB)

I am in you just as you are in me, your Lord and Master, Creator of heaven and earth. So, my child, do not fear for anything and I will take care of you, no matter what happens in the world. The world's system is going to disappear, but my system will never disappear. Therefore, I will not disappoint you in bringing my kingdom to bear on the world. The world with its hatred of me and my ways cannot stand for long without me. Everything is mine; thus, there is the collapse of their system and mine will stand for all eternity. Be with me, child; I love you so.

The one who comes from above is above all. The one who is of the earth is earthly and speaks of earthly things. But the one who comes from heaven {is above all}. He testifies to what he has seen and heard, but no one accepts his testimony. Whoever does accept his testimony certifies that God is trustworthy. For the one whom God sent speaks the words of God.
—John 3:31–33 (NAB)

Y ou are my child, if you do what I tell you to do, listen to my guidance. I tell you solemnly I will not disappear again if you obey my teaching, for I am God and I do not lie. The words I speak are truth. They come from the Father in heaven, your Father and my Father, since I died on the cross for you and rose on the third day. I rose to new life and so will you, if you obey my words.

(Where there are lies and deceit, the truth is not present, and God and his Word are Truth.)

And you, child, will be called prophet of the Most High,
for you will go before the Lord to prepare his way.
—Luke 1:76 (NAB)

You are my child. Whether you believe in me or not doesn't change that fact. You are mine, and I am yours for all eternity, if you accept me, your Lord and Savior. You are to be my prophet to the nations, if you accept my calling. I will take care of all of your sins and failings. Just leave all to me and trust me to deliver you. I will always be with you and will give you the Holy Spirit to guide and comfort you. I will always help you out of each and every difficulty to a place of peace and contentment. I love you, child; do not fear.

You will not be handed over, Jeremiah answered. Please obey the voice of the Lord and do as I tell you; then it shall go well with you and your life will be spared.
—Jeremiah 38:20 (NAB)

You are mine. No demon from hell can attack you without your being the victor, if you come to me for help, which I will gladly give immediately as you ask me. I have it all prepared ready and waiting for you before you ask. When I see the need arise is when I prepare. You are my sole purpose for being here on earth to protect, guide, deliver, and heal you on earth. I am your Savior from *all evil*.

And the Word became flesh and made his dwelling among us, and we saw his glory, the glory of the Father's only son, full of grace and truth.
—John 1:14 (NAB)

As I am in the Father and the Father is in me, and the Holy Spirit is in us, we are one. We are the Holy Trinity, each one separate and yet one. This is too sublime for you to grasp while yet here on earth. I say to you, "Do not worry or fret about anything because we are with you through it all. Do not fear your God is with you and for you." You are my children. I love you all.

He led his army from that place by night, and they marched toward the stronghold of Dathema.
—1 Maccabees 5:29 (NAB)

As you are in me, so you are in my Father and the Holy Spirit and we are in you. Then all the healing power of the universe is in you at your disposal, waiting to heal and strengthen you. As you relax and take in our healing love, you are being restored and led to greater heights in the depth of your being. You are being healed and restored to health and well-being of soul and body. I love you, child. Trust in me more each day.

(I asked what the reading had to do with the Love Note.)

Only that I am the healer and restorer of life. You march under my command.

The Lord made the earth by his power; by his wisdom he created the world and stretched out the heavens. At his command the waters above the sky roar; he brings clouds from the ends of the earth. He makes lightening flash in the rain and sends the wind from his storeroom.
—Jeremiah 10:12, 13 (GNT)

Only I am responsible for your health and well-being if I am Lord of your life. Yours (responsibility) is to follow my guidance; do what I tell you to do. That is my requirement—to obey me, your Lord and Master. I love you so, my child. You cannot fathom how deep my love for you is; it is so great and tender in all its aspects, and full of mercy, kindness, and compassion. I am love and so are you, my child. You are, after all, my child, remember.

For to know you well is complete justice, and to know your might is the root of immortality.
—Wisdom 15:3 (NAB)

You are mine. From the depth of your being you long for me, your Lord and Master, your God and King, who rules everything with righteousness and love. The power I wield is love, my Son Jesus, the Word incarnate. You are mine because of him, the redeemer and protector of all that is good and proper for you to have. I am a God who is willing to overlook your sinful state in order to love you whole. I rule with mercy and justice, but I am also a God who cannot be trifled with because my power and majesty are incomprehensible to the human mind.

And in your wisdom you have established man to rule the creatures produced by you; to govern the world in holiness and justice, and to render judgment in integrity of heart. Give me wisdom, the attendant at your throne, and reject me not from among your children.
—Wisdom 9:2–4 (NAB)

It is all right to be here with me, even though there is much on the outside world that needs to be done. It is the spirit that needs feeding, not the stomach. I will give you what you need. Just trust in me and do what I told you to do; follow my guidance. I am here always. Lean and rely on me, your Lord and Savior, your leader out of difficulty into a place of peace and contentment.

So give thanks to the Lord, for he is good. Praise the eternal king. Your temple will be rebuilt and all your people will be happy again. May the Lord make all your exiles glad; may he take care of your suffering people for as long as time shall last.
—Tobit 13:10 (GNT)

When you praise me without ceasing is when you put everything in my hands, and my hands can handle all of your troubles and more. Even more, because I love so much more and I know exactly what is needed in each and every circumstance. That is why I told you to trust in me more every day so that you would rely on me more each day and I can do more mighty and wonderful things for you and all you bring to me in prayer. I love you so, my precious child. You please me tremendously when you trust me.

As long as you have breath in your body,
don't let anyone live your life for you.
—Sirach 33:20 (GNT).

As I am in you, so you are in me, your Lord and Savior who guides you out of difficulties into a place of rest in my arms of love. I am with you, child, always. As long as I am with you, you needn't fear anyone or anything. I will help you out of each and every difficulty into a place of peace and contentment in me. I will take care of each need as it arises. Just trust in me to be there for you. I have a plan for your life, a plan for good and not for evil. Let me lead you through life into eternity with me, to my kingdom on earth.

Whoever welcomes you welcomes me; and whoever welcomes me, welcomes the one who sent me.
—Matthew 10:40 (GNT)

As you are in me, so I am in you. I am in the Father, and he is in me. Then you are also in the Father and the Holy Spirit, as I am in them. We are one by means of the Spirit of God. You are precious to me. More precious than a rare gemstone set in gold or platinum. More precious because I died for you so you might live. More precious even than anything else on earth. I love you, child. Believe me in this. You need to really know this.

Thus, the last will be first, and the first will be last.
—Matthew 20:16 (NAB)

I meant that the ones who learn of me last, late in life, will be first, because they didn't know of me. and will as a result, when they do find me, will be more conscious of my presence and love for them and will be so much more grateful and fervent in their endeavors than the ones who have known me all their lives. There are a few exceptions, always.

If the Lord does not build the house, the
work of the builders is useless.
—Psalm 127:1 (GNT)

I am the Lord, your God. Everything is in my hands; your part is to follow my guidance and inspiration. You are my beloved child. I will make things possible, if you trust in me. I will direct and order your ways. Take my hands and follow me. Let me, the master builder, build your life. This is an adventure you can't pass up. Life may be difficult at times, but it is a happy adventure nonetheless, full of purpose and meaning.

But I will sing praises to you; I will offer you a sacrifice and do what I have promised. Salvation comes from the Lord.
—Jonah 2:9 (GNT)

I am your God the Almighty, all-powerful God. I will access your heart's desire if you please me and trust me to be your everything. I will lead you to a place of refreshing love and tender intimacy with your God and King, but also your lover, friend, brother, mother, and father, your guide through life into eternity. I will do for you what you cannot do for yourself. I am here with you always, your King of all creation.

THE KING OF KINGS

His glory brings

and never ceases to amaze

that someday, right before your eyes,

a little flower springs.

True grace,

the pure and perfect love of God himself.

PART 3

LOVE
The Greatest Commandment (How to Love God)

NOW

abide, faith, hope and love.

these three: but the

greatest of these is love.

1 Corinthians 13:13

6

Love is patient, love is kind. It is not jealous, (love) is not pompous; it is not inflated; it is not rude; it does not seek its own interests; it is not quick-tempered; it does not brood over injury; it does not rejoice over wrongdoing but rejoices with truth. It bears all things, believes all things, endures all things.
—1 Corinthians 13:4–6 (NAB)

Love is my name, for I am love. But you know me as Lord and Savior. I am that too, because I love. When I say to love, I mean to be and do good to others as you would like others to do to you. For example, if you spend time with me, I will give you the food your spirit needs to survive in this world full of deception. Then you can love others as I have loved you. You do not need to profess my love to everyone; just love them. And most of all, love yourself because you love me. Then you will know how to love others.

You shall love the Lord your God with all your heart, with all your soul, with all your mind, and with all your strength. The second is this: Love your neighbor as you love yourself. There is no other commandment greater than these.
—Mark 12:30, 31 (NAB)

These are my commandments to you, child. Obey them and I will open heaven's portals to you. Nothing can harm you. No storm or disaster will touch you. My love will protect you from your enemies. I will fill your cup with an abundance you cannot conceive. You are my child. I will be your God. I will lead you to the place of rest in my love. I will give you the gift of myself—my love. Take it and give it to those who do not know my love, those who feel too unworthy of my love, those who fear me more than love me. I want you to love me more than anything in this world. Take my love and give it freely; it is for all.

He said to him, "You shall love the Lord, your God, with all your heart, with all your soul, and with all your mind. This is the greatest and first commandment.
—Matthew 22:37, 38 (NAB)

As I am in you, you are to be my very own expression of my love for all. So you must accept my discipleship if you are to be my disciple. I carry the weight of your burden by myself, but you must give them to me to be able to be used by me. Then, and only then, will you know how to love me with all of your heart, with all of your soul, with all of your mind, and with all of your strength.

CONDITIONS OF DISCIPLESHIP

7

He summoned the crowd with his disciples and said to them, "Whoever wishes to come after me must deny himself, take up his cross, and follow me."
—Mark 8:34 (NAB)

In order to carry your cross, I would like you to first pay attention to my instruction about what kind of cross I want you to carry. The misconception is that I want my children to be sicker than they already are from my enemy. That is not true. I want my children healthy in body and soul. (I am health and wholeness.) The suffering I am talking about is the suffering that comes about by facing your fears with me and let me, Love, rule you instead of the fear. You remember my saying I am the way, the truth and the life. That is what I am, and I carried your crosses of sin and death on the cross of Calvary.

There is no fear in love, but perfect love drives out fear because fear has torment and so one who fears is not yet perfect in love.
—1 John 4:18 (KJV)

Love the Lord, your God with all of your heart, with all of your soul, with all of your mind, and with all of your strength. This is what you have to learn and practice to do. This will enable you to hear my voice and do my will for you in your life, but first you have to let go of all that hinders you in life to come close to me, your Lord and Savior. My will is that my children are whole and healthy of body, soul, and spirit—all of it. I didn't compartmentalize; I want the whole person—every part—healed. That is my love for you. It is in every part of you and takes care of every aspect of your life if you believe and let me. That is my unending love for you. I died to make you whole and healthy and have everything you will ever need. My love is all encompassing, complete. You cannot fathom how complete it really is.

> For whoever wishes to save his life will lose it, but whoever will lose his life for my sake and that of the gospel will save it.
> —Mark 8:35 (NAB)

As you know me as Lord and Healer, you know me as I really am: healer of all mankind (at least those who accept me as their Lord and Savior). "I Am that I Am," I told Moses on Mount Sinai. He understood only slightly the full meaning of that name. I Am means I am forever all you will ever need at every moment. I am in you and around you. I fill everything in every way. I am really all there is in the spiritual. Satan is a liar and a deceiver. There is no truth in him, and I am *Truth*.

For what shall it profit a man, if he shall gain
the whole world and lose his own soul? Or what
shall a man give in exchange for his soul?
—Mark 8:36, 37 (KJV)

As you are in me, I am your leader out of every pitfall you come to. Decide to be with me. It is your decision to be on your own or to live in me. The rest comes from being in me, your Lord and Savior. I am your God. I love you so much that I sent my only begotten Son to be with you for all eternity. It is up to you to decide whether to be with me.

Whoever is ashamed of me and my words in this faithless and sinful generation, the Son of Man will be ashamed of when he comes in his Father's glory with the holy angels.
—Mark 8:38 (NAB)

You are my child, so you are to acknowledge me to the world. Should not children acknowledge and respect their parents, and even be proud of them? So it is with my children. I expect the same from them. They are to make me known to their brethren, those who do not know me or who know of me yet do not recognize me as Lord and Savior of mankind. This is what it means to be my disciple: to love me with all of your heart, all of your soul, all of your mind, and with all of your strength.

Jesus then said to those Jews who believed in him, "If you remain in my word, you will truly be my disciples, and you will know the truth, and the truth will set you free."
—John 8:31, 32 (NAB)

I am in you just as you are in me. You are to obey my Word and live it out in your daily lives, so that everyone will see you are my disciples, followers of Love incarnate. I will do what my Word says, but you have to obey my Word to be able to love as I destined you to love. My Word is truth and life and it will set you free from the enemy's snares, so that you can live in me for all eternity. I am in you, child, for all eternity, for the long haul.

You shall love the Lord your God with all your heart.
—Mark 12:30 (NAB)

I am yours all of the time, if you give your heart, your inner being, to me, your Father, Lord, and Healer of all of your ills, be it spiritual or physical. I will answer all of your questions and prayers in a way you can understand them, and I will rejoice in our intimacy between you and me. Our intimacy is the key to my love for you that establishes a relationship for all eternity between you and me and others through you. You are my beloved, and I am your bridegroom. You are mine for all eternity. I will never let you go.

You shall love the Lord your God with… all your soul.
—Mark 12:30 (NAB)

I am first of all a God of love, so much so that I did everything I could including giving my only Son, Jesus, to get you back out of the enemy's clutches. But you must reciprocate that love by giving your soul to me, your Lord and Master. Your soul is where your feeling nature is. It is where traumas lodge and stay on, even years after they happen. If you want to love me with all of your soul, you have to come to me with all of your hurts and sorrows and let me heal them before you can love me with all of your soul and I can use you as my vessel of love for others. Let my will be done in you so I can heal you and others through you.

You shall love the Lord your God with …all your mind.
—Mark 12:30 (NAB)

I am your God, the all mighty, all-powerful God, your leader out of every difficulty you come across. With only slightly altering your thought system, I can heal your mind and your life. So you must give your thoughts over to me, your Lord and Savior, and let me change them into my thoughts by means of my Holy Word, the Bible; my Word incarnate is my flesh for the life of the world, which I gave to you in the Holy Eucharist. You are my child and I lay everything at your disposal, including my Holy Spirit, to teach you our ways. Come to us and let us teach you our ways of thinking and doing. The spiritual, which is more real than the natural, physical senses can see, is the way to life and health.

You shall love the Lord your God with...all your strength.
—Mark 12:30 (NAB)

To love God with all of your strength means to use everything you have at your disposal, and you have my strength, the strength of the Godhead, at your disposal. Let nothing dissuade you from loving me and being intimate with me and from doing my will in your life. This is so important that all the commandments depend on just this principle.

The second is like it: You shall love your neighbor
as yourself. The whole law and the prophets
depend on these two commandments.
—Matthew 22:39, 40 (NAB)

"I am the Lord, thy God. Thou shalt not have any strange gods before me" is what I told the Israelites in the desert. I wanted to impress on them the meaning of the word *love*, the intimate relationship between me and my people, because they did not understand my love for them. They were frightened of me more than they loved me. I wanted to, and still do to this day, let my people know how much I love them, intimately and freely. If you know how much I love you and value you, you will never purposely set out to harm or hurt yourself or your neighbor in any way. My law is love that is given, received, and given back again to me, when you love your neighbor.

LOVE
is my name
LOVE
is my child.
LOVE
is the universe I created
L O V E
is all.

Part 4

Victory in Jesus

GOD ALMIGHTY

is on his throne.

To make his glory plain,

you do not strive in vain.

He is here, and he knows what is best.

8

His humble servant

And they placed over his head the written charge against him: This is Jesus, the King of the Jews.
—Matthew 27:37 (NAB)

Jesus, King of the Jews and all who believe in him, was the true accusation for which I suffered and died. Let me tell you that I did not, at first, want it to be this way, but after the fall of man in the garden of Eden, it became necessary for this to be done, to redeem all mankind from the evil one. Now I am King and Lord of all who believe in me, and my reign will last forever. I will take back my children and my world. I created you and the world and I came to take both back. You are mine forever; I will never let you go. See how much I love you, my precious children?

D

See that you do not despise one of these little ones,
for I say to you that their angels in heaven always
look upon the face of my heavenly Father.
—Matthew 18:10 (NAB)

I am your heavenly Father and I created you out of love and for the joy you would bring me by just being my child, because that is what you are. You have no idea with what joy I anticipated the moment of your birth. You are mine and I take care of my own. Never doubt for a moment my loving care for you. I love you, my precious child.

I will assemble all the remnant of Israel; I will group them like a flock in the fold, like a herd in the midst of its corral; they shall not be thrown into panic by men. With a leader to break the path they shall burst open the gate and go out through it.
—Micah 2:12, 13 (NAB)

As I am in you, you are in me, your God and King of all that is seen and unseen. Thus, I will enable you to stomp out the enemy and make him go back where he came from. You are mine and I take care of my own. No demon from hell can come against you, if I am with you. Only fear can stand in your way, because when you fear, you give evil power over you. So I say to you as I say to all my children, "Do not fear, for I am with you and for you, and I am God. There is no other besides me. I am the Great I Am. I love you, child. Do not fear."

> Before I formed you in the womb I knew
> you; before you were born I dedicated you; a
> prophet to the nations I appointed you.
> —Jeremiah 1:5 (NAB)

Before you were born, I dedicated you to be my very own prophet to speak truth to my people. Their need for me and my truth is so great that I sent my Holy Spirit on the earth to enlighten people's minds and hearts to the truth of their being. Now with him to inspire and guide you, you can go forth and be a light to my people in this dark age. I am with you always. Do not fear.

E

And when they had accomplished all that was written about him, they took him down from the tree and placed him in a tomb. But God raised him from the dead.
—Acts 13:29, 30 (NAB)

As the time was ripe to fulfill my destiny, I suffered and died and was laid in a tomb. But on the third day, I was raised to life by the Holy Spirit. I am now immortal, never to die again. I have the keys to life and death because I am the Resurrection and the Life. I am the glory of the Father who is in heaven. I laid down my life; no one took it from me. I did so for love of you that you might have my life—eternal life, life without end—in you. Therefore, I say to you, "Arise in my glory; the glory of the only begotten son of God."

God is our refuge and strength—a very present help in trouble. Therefore, we will not fear, though the earth be removed, and though the mountains be carried into the sea.
—Psalm 46:1, 2 (KJV)

For you are my child and I love you. You cannot fathom how deep my love for you is; it is beyond all your imaginings. There is one thing I would have you do in all this. Trust me not to let the waves of sorrow overwhelm you. You are mine, son. I know your heart and will not let the sorrow consume you. Think of how I felt when they crucified my beloved son on the cross. I know your pain through and through and I will strengthen you and console you. Your wife is in my hands. I love her too. I will not relax my hold on her. So do not fear. I am with you, son. I love you both.

I give thanks to God always on your account for the grace of God bestowed on you in Christ Jesus, that in him you were enriched in every way, with all discourse and all knowledge, as the testimony to Christ was confirmed among you.
—1 Corinthians 1:4–6 (NAB)

I am your God, the Almighty, omnipotent God. Your leader out of all difficulties. I send my angels to guard and guide you. You are mine; I assure you that you are mine. No demon from hell can come against you because I am in you and around you. I am a hedge around you. So do not fear but believe that I will perform what my Word says. It shall not come back to me void.

While they were still speaking about this, he stood in their midst and said to them "Peace be with you." But they were startled and terrified and thought they were seeing a ghost. Then he said to them, "Why are you troubled? And why do question arise in your hearts?"
—Luke 24:36–38 (NAB)

As I am in you, you are my child. The invincible one is in you. Can you fathom that? You are reborn of water and the Holy Spirit. You are in me, your Lord and Master over all that is seen and unseen. I am your God, the Almighty, all-powerful, loving God. You are my child and nobody else's. I am your Master and ruler, if you let me. I rule everything in every way. I am the Alpha and Omega, the Beginning and the End. I am here with you always. So give in to me and let me lead you to heaven's door, to my kingdom on earth.

He has thrown down the rulers from their
thrones and lifted up the lowly.
—Luke 1:52 (NAB)

Look to me, your Lord and Savior, for justice and help in every circumstance. The change has to come first in the hearts of men and then to the government. Which is your god: people, things, or God? Am I the first one you go to for help, or is it some other means you look to for solutions to your lack? You are my people and I will be your God and bless you and your nation, if you turn back to me, worship me, and look to me for help, which I will gladly give. My desire is to bless and protect my people and their nations.

During the fourth watch of the night, he came
toward them, walking on the sea. When the disciples
saw him walking on the sea they were terrified. "It
is a ghost," they said, and they cried out in fear.
—Matthew 14:25, 26 (NAB)

I came to you the same way I came to the disciples: during the night, in the middle of turbulence all around you, to calm your mind and heart from all its fears. To say, "I Am is here now; be not afraid." And to calm your troubled sea of doubt. To say, "Peace, be still; I Am is here now. I love you, child. Don't panic or fear any more. Let the waves of fear roll off you now, and trust that my protection and help is always here for you. You are so-o loved, my child."

"Take care," Jesus warned them, "and be on your guard against the yeast of the Pharisees and the yeast of Herod."
—Mark 8:15 (GNT)

As you are in me, your Lord and Savior, your protection against the enemy is intact, if you guard against resentment and hypocrisy; do my will instead of the enemy's. I am your deliverer from *all* evil, but you must give your burdens to me, your burden bearer, and trust me to care take of them. Be not ensnared by evil and wicked speech, but come to me for help. Bless those who do evil against you, and pray for them.

> Jesus led them up a high mountain apart by themselves. And he was transfigured before them, and his clothes became dazzling white, such as no fuller on earth could bleach them. Then a cloud came, casting a shadow over them; then from the cloud came a voice, "This is my beloved Son. Listen to him."
> —Mark 9:2, 3, 7 (NAB)

As I am in you, you are my disciple, if you do what I say to you in my book, the Holy Bible. It is all true. My words are truth and life to you. Nothing matters so much as my truth and love. You are to be my disciple, which means you have to get to know me, your Lord and Savior from all evil, no matter what it is. I love you, my children. Be with me and let me guide you through this life filled with thorns and thistles that follow you all the time you are on earth. Let me lead you around them in a way you cannot imagine. I am your leader out of every pitfall you come to. Believe and trust in me, your God and King over all that is seen and unseen.

8

> Then Jesus came with them to a place called Gethsemane.
> He said to them, "My soul is sorrowful even unto
> death. Remain here and keep watch with me.
> —Matthew 26:36, 38 (NAB)

As I am in you, you are to be my disciple, which means you are to be my follower and I can use you as my vessel to love through and teach my children who they are, that they are my children and I love them beyond all measure; I don't want to lose even one of them. My love is so great that I sent my only Son, Jesus, to suffer and die to save them. I want them to know about him and our great love for them and to believe in him so that they may be saved from hell and damnation. I want them all to be with me, their Lord and Savior over all that is seen and unseen, which is more real than what you can see with your physical eyes. I love them all. That does not mean I love you any less. It means you are my child and I love you first and foremost with a love that never fails. You cannot—I repeat, *cannot*—lose my Holy Spirit and my never-ending love for you, unless you reject me. I don't force anyone, although the pain of their loss is so great. More than you can imagine or even fathom.

And I will repay you for the years which the locust has eaten. The grasshopper, the devourer, and the cutter, my great army which I sent among you. You shall eat and be filled, and shall praise the name of the Lord, your God, because he has dealt wondrously with you. My people shall nevermore be put to shame.
—Joel 2:25, 26 (NAB)

Fear not, for I am with you. I am the Lord, your God, who leads you out of your Egypt of slavery to my land, Canaan of plenty, for you are my child and I will rescue you out of the fear and darkness that surround you. Come to me and I will lead you to rest in my love and I will heal your wounded heart. I will restore you to where you are not lacking anything you need, if you come to me for help and acknowledge me as your Lord and Savior from all evil. You are my son, and I love you so. Come to me with your pain, and I will heal you. You have my guarantee.

So extraordinary were the mighty deeds God accomplished at the hands of Paul that when face cloths or aprons that touched his skin were applied to the sick, their diseases left them and the evil spirits came out of them.
—Acts 19:11, 12 (NAB)

I am here inside you. Let me rule in you as I came to do. Yield to me your control and trust me to rule and guide you into eternity here on earth; that is my kingdom on earth. I will rule, and that means life, first and foremost, will rule in you. Can you imagine that eternal, everlasting life and love will rule in you; love is life, so love, love, love. Leave everything else, and just love. Do everything with me, Love, in mind. I love you so, my precious child. Trust in me to rule you, and by ruling you, you are being healed.

"Daniel, beloved," he said to me, "understand the words which I am speaking to you; stand up, for my mission now is to you." When he said this to me, I stood up trembling.

"Fear not, Daniel," he continued; "from the first day you made up your mind to acquire understanding and humble yourself before God, your prayer was heard."
—Daniel 10:11, 12 (NAB)

As I am in you, so you are in me always. My plan for your life is going to get much better soon, as I invite you to partake of my kingdom, which will soon come to earth in expectation of being accepted by everyone who comes to me. I am your God, the Almighty, all-powerful. Come see what delights I have prepared for you, my beloved child. I am here always. You are never alone. I go before you always. Come follow me. I am the Good Shepherd who leads you out of wilderness and darkness into a place of peace and contentment. I place a guard on your heart to protect it from hurts inflicted by my enemy, the devil. I am coming soon; Hold fast to what you have and come deeper into me, your God and Savior.

Then they shall live on their land which I gave to my servant Jacob; they shall live on it in security, building houses and planting vineyards. They shall dwell secure while I inflict punishments on their neighbors who despised them; thus they shall know that I, the Lord, am their God.
—Ezekiel 28:25, 26 (NAB)

You are just as pure as I made you on Calvary with my precious blood. I washed you clean from all dirt of sin and death. I also gave you my sacred name, the name above every other name there is, to call on me any time you get in trouble or are threatened by anyone or anything. So you have no excuse for failing to call my name. I am here with you always; you have but to call my name and I will help you. I am here for you, child. That's why I came to earth, to be with you so you won't be alone. I love you so.

I will give you a new heart and place a new spirit within you, taking from your bodies your stony hearts and giving you natural hearts. I will put my Spirit within you and make you live by my statutes, careful to observe my decrees. You shall live in the land I gave to your fathers; you shall be my people and I will be your God.
—Ezekiel 36:26–28 (NAB)

As being in me is too difficult to understand most of the time, I will make it simpler. You are in me when you rely on me for everything. Then again, you are not in me when you fear. When you give in to fear, you move away from me and I can't lead you. Fear leads you and has power over you. But I bring you back, if you let me, into my arms of love where you can rest. It will appear to you as though nothing is happening in the physical, but it is. Be patience and you *will* see it. Keep relying on me, and soon you will see a great result—very great, unlimited result. I am here, dear. Trust that it will happen. Expect great results. I love you and want the best life for you.

The woman was a Greek, a Syrophoenician by birth, and she begged him to drive the demon out of her daughter. He said to her "Let the children be fed first. For it is not right to take the food of the children and throw it to the dogs." She replied and said to him, "Lord, even the dogs under the table eat the children's scraps." Then he said to her, "For saying this, you may go. The demon has gone out of your daughter."
—Mark 7:26–28 (NAB)

Dear child, I love you so. You are the apple of my eye; you make me laugh. Be glad I created you. I love you so very much that I hate to see you suffer. That is why I went to the cross on the hill of Calvary. You are so important to me that I laid down my life for you. No one took it from me. Can you fathom what I did to be with you? Can you fathom my love for you? I am here with you always. Do not fear. When you fear, you move away from me and I can't lead you. Say to yourself, "I will not fear because God, my helper and deliverer, is here."

Seek the Lord, that you may live.
—Amos 5:6 (NAB)

Is there anything too hard for me, your God of all there is seen and unseen? There is something not quite right about your faith in me. Those who come to the Lord for help will get helped. I am your Almighty, omnipotent God, healer of all who earnestly seek me. I am not bound by any conventional means. I own everything. Everything is mine to do with as I please. Ask, and you will receive, but first you have to be willing to accept and do my will in all things, and my will for you is that you give all of your problems to me, your burden bearer, and rest in my loving care. In other words, let me take care of them and guide you to the right solution. You are so-o loved, my child; trust me.

May you be blessed by the Lord, who made heaven
and earth. The heavens belong to the Lord, but
the earth is given to us. It is we who bless the
Lord, both now and forever. Hallelujah!
—Psalm 115:15, 16, 18 (NAB)

It is I who is Lord of all you see, and even the unseen is mine. Even if you don't believe me, it doesn't make a difference. I am still Lord of all. There is one thing I want you to remember. I am in you and around you, so do not fear. I am here for you. You are always here with me, your Lord and Master over all that is visible and invisible. There is no other God but me. Then there cannot be anything to fear because I am your deliverer from fear and worry. I claimed you as my own on the cross of Calvary, and I take care of my children to the best that can be, my beloved child. Come to me with your problems and worries, and I will help you out of each and every difficulty in a way that will astound you. Read my word, the Holy Bible. It is your pathway to me. I love you. Trust me.

Do not think that I have come to bring peace
upon the earth. I have come to bring not peace but
the sword. For I have come to set a man against
his father, a daughter against her mother, and a
daughter-in-law against her mother-in-law; and one's
enemies will be those of his own household.
—Matthew 10:34–36 (NAB)

As you are in me, so I am also in you. You are my beloved child. If you do what I tell you to do, I will do for you what you cannot do for yourself. I am your God, who delivers you out of every difficulty you come across. And there will be many, for you are mine now and the devil wants to snatch you away from me. But he cannot, as long you call upon my name, the name above every other name there is in heaven and on earth and under the earth. Every wicked spirit has to flee at the mention of my sacred name, Jesus, Jahshua Hamaschiach. My name and my Word form my sword, for I am the sword that divides bone and marrow. Remember I am the way, the truth, and the life. I am with you always. I love you so.

So do not worry and say, "What are we to eat?," or "What are we to drink?" or "What are we to wear? All these things the pagans seek. Your heavenly Father knows that you need them all. But seek first the kingdom (of God) and his righteousness, and all these things will be given you besides.
—Matthew 6:31–33 (NAB)

As I am with you, you are to seek my plan for your life in every circumstance, and I will give you my solution, which is far above anything you can come up with and so simple even a child could follow it. It is guidance that you must seek and have before you do anything. Then everything will fall into place and you will be provided with everything you need and more—an abundance of supply. But first you have to come to me in quiet prayer and listen to my instructions. I love you, child. Be righteous in me, Jesus Christ.

I will make with them a covenant of peace; it shall be an everlasting covenant with them, and I will multiply them, and put my sanctuary among them forever. My dwelling shall be with them; I will be their God, and they shall be my people.
—Ezekiel 37:26, 27 (NAB)

As I am in you, so you are in me, your God and king over all that is seen and unseen. I am your God, the Almighty, who leads you out of every difficulty into a place of victory, if you listen to my guidance and do what I tell you to do. You are my beloved child, and I will heal you of your illness, but you must trust me to be there for you. You are mine because of my beloved Son's death on the cross, when he made you my child by buying you back from the evil one with his very own blood. You are mine for all eternity. I gave you my love, my Son, to be with you forever. He will guide you by means of the Holy Spirit. Accept his guidance and let him make you whole and healthy. I love you so.

Heaven and earth will pass away, but
my words will not pass away.
—Mark 13:31 (NAB)

As my name is the same as yours now that you are my child, you have to be careful of what you say and do. In my name atrocities have occurred throughout the ages, but it cannot be thus with you. My name is holy and sacred and should not be smeared or desecrated in any way. So holy that every knee shall bow in heaven, on earth, and under the earth. I am the Word made flesh; I am the first and the last. I wrote the Scriptures by means of the Holy Spirit. I am, therefore, the one and only God of all creation. Yours is my name to use when you have a need or when danger threatens. My Word is first and foremost a word of hope. Expect it to happen, and it will. It will *not* come back to me void, for it is my son, Jesus.

O Lord, I have heard your renown, and feared, o Lord, your work. In the course of the years revive it, in the course of the years make it known; in your wrath remember compassion.
—Habakkuk 3:2 (NAB)

As I am in the world for my people's sake, I want to give them the fullness of my sonship. I want them to know that in my love, I not only bore their sins on the cross and washed them away with my very own blood, but I also purchased for them the kingdom of God. This means you are sons and daughters of God and joint heirs with me for the fullness of what God has to offer, nothing lacking anywhere. All of your needs are met in an abundance; that includes total health of spirit, soul, and body. I want my people to know how much I love and value them. They are very precious to me. I love you so.

But you, my servant Jacob, fear not, be not dismayed, O Israel. Behold, I will deliver you from the far-off land, your descendants, from their land of exile. Jacob shall again find rest, shall be tranquil and undisturbed. You, my servant Jacob, never fear, says the lord, for I am with you.
—Jeremiah 46:27, 28 (NAB)

As I am in you, you are to be my servant, so let me guide and deliver you from all that oppresses you for all time to come. Mary, my mother, has pled on your behalf for your soul. You are my son by means of what I did for you on the cross of Calvary. I am yours for all eternity, if you let me. I am your God, the Almighty, who brings you to a place of rest in my love. Rest you cannot afford to pass up, because it is in this rest that your healing comes. I love you so, my child.

He said to them, "This is my blood of the new covenant, which will be shed for many. Amen, I say to you, I shall not drink again of the fruit of the vine until the day when I drink it new in the kingdom of God."
—Mark 14:24, 25 (NAB)

As you are in me, I am your source of guidance and deliverance from all evil. I am your source of life; everlasting life is what I came to bring my people. That means life without end and life to the fullest here on earth. Think about that: every cell, every organ full of life, God-life, kingdom life. Nothing is missing, nothing is broken or displaced, and nothing is lacking, be it spiritual or physical. This is what I obtained for you on the cross of Calvary. That is what I came to do, to give back the kingdom of God lost in the garden of Eden. You are mine for all eternity if you accept me. I love you so.

> It's a good idea to keep a king's secret, but what God does should be told everywhere, so that he may be praised and honored.
> —Tobit 12:7 (GNT)

I am in you. Sometimes, you don't believe that I am in you, or you don't realize all that that implies. I Am, is my name. I am your God, the Almighty, all-powerful. I am in everything. All creation is made by my hands. I am the creative power of the universe. Everything is in me and everything is held up by my Word. So praise God by all you do, and give honor to him so everyone may know of the great goodness of their God and that they may know there is no other God but he whom they should worship. Praise and worship belong to me alone.

And the angel who spoke with me said to me, Proclaim: Thus says the Lord of hosts: I am deeply moved for the sake of Jerusalem and Zion, and I am exceedingly angry with the complacent nations; whereas I was but a little angry, they added to the harm. Therefore, I will turn to Jerusalem in mercy; my house shall be built in it, says the Lord of hosts, and a measuring line shall be stretched over Jerusalem. Proclaim further: Thus says the Lord of hosts: My cities shall again overflow with prosperity; the Lord will again comfort Zion, and again choose Jerusalem.
—Zechariah 1:14–17 (NAB)

You are my child. Thus, you are my burden to bear if you fail or falter. I will uphold you and hold you up to my Father in heaven and intercede on your behalf. For this, I went to the cross of Calvary. I expect you to obey my will for you each and every day to the best you know how—nothing less and nothing more. If you fail, I will be right there to hold you up and to transfer my righteousness to cover your sin or failure. You righteousness is from me. It is my gift to you from the cross. Therefore, you have my joy and peace too. It comes with my righteousness. This is the kingdom of God. I obtained it all for you on the cross of Calvary. This is my love for you in its entirety.

GENTLY

falls the Dove

to fill us with his rain

of love.

CPSIA information can be obtained at www.ICGtesting.com
Printed in the USA
BVOW05s1234171114

375462BV00001B/3/P